Herbert Walther

The
12th SS Armored
Division

A Documentation in Words and Pictures

Schiffer Publishing Ltd

1469 Morstein Road, West Chester, Pennsylvania 19380

List of Waffen-SS Ranks and their World War 2 German and US Equivalents

Waffen SS	German WW 2 Army	US WW 2 Army
General Officers		
—no equivalent—	Generalfeldmarschall	General of the Army
Oberstgruppenführer	Generaloberst	General
Obergruppenführer	General	Lieutenant General
Gruppenführer	Generalleutnant	Major General
Brigadeführer	Generalmajor	Brigadier General
Staff Officers		
Oberführer	—no equivalent—	—no equivalent—
	(wore the shoulder strap of a colonel)	
Standartenführer	Oberst	Colonel
Obersturmbannführer	Oberstleutnant	Lieutenant Colonel
Sturmbannführer	Major	Major
Company Officers		
Hauptsturmführer	Hauptmann	Captain
Obersturmführe	Oberleutnant	1st Lieutenant
Untersturmführer	Leutnant	2nd Lieutenant
Officer Candidates (basically equal to Oberfeldwebel & Feldwebel)		
Oberjunker	Oberfähnrich	—no equivalent—
Junker	Fähnrich	—no equivalent—
Noncommissioned Officers		
Sturmscharführer	Stabsfeldwebel	Sergeant Major
Oberscharführer	Oberfeldwebel	Master Sergeant
Scharführer	Feldwebel	Technical Sergeant
Unterscharführer	Unterfeldwebel	Staff Sergeant
	Unterofficier	Sergeant
Enlisted Men		
—no equivalent—	Stabsgefreiter	Admin Corporal
Rottenführer	Obergetfreiter	Corporal
Sturmmann	Geffreiter	Corporal
SS-Obersoldt *	Obersoldt *	Private 1st Class
SS-Soldat *	Soldat *	Private

*Note: "Soldat" is a general term. Other words used here are Schütze, Grenadier, Füsilier, depending upon the combat arm to which the soldier belonged.

Source of US World War 2 army equivalents: War Department Technical Manual TM-E 30-451 *Handbook on German Military Forces*, 15 March 1945.

Copyright © 1989 by Herbert Walther.
Library of Congress Catalog Number: 88-64000.

Translated from German by Dr. Edward Force.
Printed in the United States of America.
ISBN: 0-88740-166-X
Published by Schiffer Publishing Ltd.
1469 Morstein Road, West Chester, Pennsylvania 19380

This book may be purchased from the publisher.
Please include $2.00 postage.
Try your bookstore first.

FOREWORD

Although literature about the 12th SS Armored Division "Hitler Youth" ("HJ") and its service at the front already exists in German, English and French, this new volume is meant to document in only 120 pages, and in an impressive, comprehensible way, the fate of this division, and above all its formation and its defeat in the defensive fighting around Caen.

After having written three books about the Waffen SS and thus mentioning the "HJ" Division appropriately, I feel that, after finishing my book on the 1st Armored Division "Bodyguard", the "HJ" Division should naturally follow as the next volume in the new series.

As a Junior Company Leader and Ordnance Officer in the 12th SS Regiment "HJ", I was in service from the beginning of the invasion fighting to the outbreak from the basin at Falaise.

In those months it was my duty to maintain connections not only from the staff of Section II of the 12th SS Regiment to the armored companies and the infantry units subordinate to them, but also to the staffs, armored regiment, division, and SS Armored Corps I. This work provided me at that time with good insights and contacts on all levels. All of this was later expanded through study of the appropriate sources, especially those of the other side. I relied on the "War History of the 12th SS Armored Division HJ", probably the most thorough account of the service of a German division, written by the former Ia Hubert Meyer, the book "Grenadiers" by "Panzermeyer", which appeared as early as 1956, the book "Wearers of the Knight's Cross in the Waffen SS" by Günter Kretschmer, and the book "Third Company", a genuine group creation by the men of the "Ribbentrop Company" (3rd SS Armored Regiment 12).

From the Allied side, I used above all "The defeat of the Rommel Army Group" by Alexander McKee, "Six Armies in Normandy" by John Keegen, the book in the Elite No. 2 series published by Orbis Publishing of London, as well as the two exhaustive Heimdal Editions volumes of photographs "Les Panzers" and "Normandie-Album Memorial" by Georges Bernage and Dr. Jean-Pierre Benamou.

Several visits to the battlefields around Caen, including those with the veterans of the II. Section, Armored Regiment 12, and by invitation of the Sunday Express on the occasion of the fortieth anniversary of the Allied invasion, have refreshed my knowledge and memory.

The photographs taken by SS War Reporter Wilfried Woscidlo, who served with the "HJ" Division, as well as by other Army and Air Force reporters, were enhanced by pictures which comrades placed at my disposal, above all Peter Witt, from those that he inherited from his father.

Many photographs from the Imperial War Museum of London document the service of Britons and Canadians. The color photographs, mainly also those of W. Woscidlo, are for the most part unpublished. They are naturally subject to the conditions of photography in the fifth year of the war, but in their own particular way they bear evidence to the service of the 12th SS Armored Division "HJ".

I hope that I have succeeded in documenting and honoring the sacrifice of these young volunteers, their service in good faith, in the proper way.

Herbert Walther

ACKNOWLEDGEMENTS

The author wishes to thank Meinrad Nilges and Werner Held of the Federal Archives, Koblenz, the colleagues of the Imperial War Museum, London, Mr. Jost W. Schneider, Wuppertal, Mr. Georges Bernage, Editions Heimdal, Bayeux, and Dr. Jean Pierre Benamou, Caen, as well as the many friends and comrades, particularly Peter Witt, Hans Siegel and Herbert Höfler. I have my dear wife Alice to thank for her cooperation, help and patience.

PHOTO SOURCES

Federal Archives, Koblenz
Imperial War Museum, London
Archives of Jost W. Schneider,
Wuppertal
Archives of Editions Heimdal,
Bayeux
and photos from private sources

CONTENTS

COMMANDERS

Fritz Witt
Military Career

3/17/1933	Entry into the LAH
10/ 1/1933	2nd Lieutenant
5/ 9/1934	1st Lieutenant
1/12/1935	Transfer to "Deutschland" Guard, Company Leader, 3rd SS "Deutschland"
7/ 1/1935	Captain
10/16/1940	Retransfer to LAH as Commander, Third Battalion
3/26/1941	Commander, First Battalion of the LAH
11/17/1941	Lieutenant Colonel
1/30/1943	Colonel
7/ 1/1943	Oberführer, Commander, "HJ" Division
4/20/1944	Brigadier General

Military Honors

9/17/1939	Iron Cross Second Class
9/26/1939	Iron Cross First Class
9/ 4/1940	Knight's Cross
Feb. 1942	German Cross in Gold
3/ 1/1943	Oak Leaf Cluster to Knight's Cross

Born in Hohenlimburg on May 27, 1908.
Fell June 14, 1944, at his division's position in Caen-Vernoix. His last resting place is in the Military Cemetery of St. Andre-de-l'Eure.

SS Brigadier General Freitz Witt directed the formation and training of the 12th SS Armored Division "Hitler Youth" and commanded them in the decisive first days of the defensive battle around Caen, until the grenades of a ship's weaponry ended this soldier's life.

Fritz Witt as Commander of the 3rd Corps SS "Deutschland", at the head of a guard of honor in Munich, November 9, 1936.

Home on furlough, Christmas 1940, with daughter and son Peter.

In the summer of 1941 on the march into Russia; in front is the Commander of the 1st Corps of the LAH, Gerd Pleiss, who fell soon afterward in the fighting around Rostov.

Fritz Witt, by now a Colonel with
Oak Leaf Cluster, in the fighting
around Kharkov, March, 1943.

On his 37th and last birthday with
his loyal companion, his shepherd
dog "Bulli".

Fritz Witt as Brigadier General with
the Commander of the First SS
Armored Corps, Sepp Dietrich, who
wears a black Panzer uniform.

The first grave of Fritz Witt in the
park of Chateaux de la Guillerie, in
Tillieres sur Avre.

Kurt Meyer as a Captain, Chief of
the 15th Motorcycle Company of
the LAH, on the Western Front,
summer 1940.

"Panzermeyer" as Commander of the
Reconnaissance Section of the LAH, in the
ancient stadium of Olympia, April 1941.

On June 14, 1944, the former Commander of
the 25th SS Armored Grenadier Regiment,
Kurt Meyer, known to all as "Panzermeyer",
took command of the "Hitler Youth
Division"; at 33 he was the youngest division
commander in the German Army.

In the fighting around Kharkov he was
honored with the Oak Leaf Cluster to the
Knight's Cross (2/23/1943). With him in this
picture of a long discussion are the
commanders who soon thereafter assumed
important assignments in the formation of
the "HJ" Division and were to see service
later. From left to right: Fritz Witt, Max
Wünsche, "Panzermeyer" (concealing
Division Surgeon Besuden of the LAH).

Reception after the Battle of
Kharkov by Empire Minister Dr.
Goebbels. Kurt Meyer with his
successor in command of the "HJ"
Division, Hugo Kraas. From left to
right: Jünttner, "Panzermeyer",
Wünnsche, Dr. Goebbels, Hugo
Kraas.

Kurt Meyer, at left in the picture, by now a
Colonel and Commander of the SS Armored
Grenadier Regiment 25, with Gerd Bremer,
formerly Section Leader and Company
Commander under him, seen here in the summer
of 1944 as Commander of the AA of the 12th SS
Armored Division "HJ".

At left Hugo Kraas, a worthy leader, who was
also one of the first to join the "Bodyguard" in
1933. In the war he served as Company
Commander, Battalion Commander and
Regiment Commander in the LAH, until on
November 15, 1944 he became Commander of the
12th SS Armored Division "HJ" and led it till the
bitter end.

11

HITLER YOUTH AND
PRE-MILITARY TRAINING

After Hitler came to power on January 30, 1933, German youth did not flock to the Hitler Youth. The many youth groups that grew out of the Wandervogel movement, youth groups of the soldiers' organizations, political parties and religious groups, were, on the contrary, determined not to be unified into the "HJ" (Hitler Jugend "Hitler Youth"), which in the end they were unable to prevent. Probably the last strong demonstration of the German youth organizations is shown in this picture of their color guards marching past Admiral von Trotha at the Skaggerak Festival in Berlin on May 28, 1933. By no means all of the young leaders who are watching the march are saluting with raised arm.

Jugend dient dem Führer

ALLE ZEHNJÄHRIGEN IN DIE HJ.

It took a lot more drumming in every sense to get young people marching in the new direction, often by force.

At the age of ten the "wolf cubs" joined the "German Young Folk", at fourteen they were taken into the "Hitler Youth", and at eighteen into the NSDAP (Nazi Party). This took place automatically, thus after the war many had to defend themselves against the charge of having been party members, although this membership was "dealt out" to them.

"Who has the youth, has the future": thus everything was set up to inspire the young, and soon they all sang the "Hitler Youth" song together. In the process, very few gave any thought to the fateful line in the refrain: "The flag is more than death".

Pre-military training was slowly introduced into their teaching and their evenings at home. What boy would not have been inspired?

A few chosen ones were allowed to carry the flags to Nürnberg for the youth rally at Reich Party Day. Here Adolf Hitler made known to them what he wanted "his" youth to be: "Slim and slender they should be, tough as leather, hard as Krupp steel and fast as greyhounds".

There was also the great chance to acquire practical wisdom in the "Special Units", as in the "Marine HJ" or the "Motor HJ", where the theory and practice of transport training could be concluded by a driving test.

The "Flyer HJ" naturally was an especially strong lure to young people who intended to go into the Air Force. Here they built their own models and training gliders.

Best of all was, of course, a solo flight under the direction of experienced instructors.

In the "News HJ" training was done with the most modern apparatus. In the picture at the upper right, the boys are, in 1939, already using a Siemens-Hell Field Teletype. Here too, the purpose of the training is clearly its later use in armed forces communications.

At the beginning of the war, intensive training was carried out in the "Warrior Capability Camps" under the direction of experienced military specialists.

Above: Ski training in the mountains.

Below: Training in the use of maps in preparation for a terrain exercise.

More and more junior officers of
the SS were used as instructors in
the Warrior Capability Camps.

Here the intended purpose was obvious:
to recruit volunteers for service in the
Waffen SS. Particular emphasis was placed
on marksmanship training.

When Adolf Hitler commanded in 1943 that a division be established from the ranks of the "HJ", the need was naturally very great. Volunteers were solicited for entrance into this fully new unit among the "HJ" organization and particularly in the Warrior Capability Camps. The senior and junior leaders came chiefly from the First SS Armored Division "Bodyguard" (LAH). Former "HJ" leaders already in the army were utilized as well. The two divisions were to form the newly created First SS Armored Corps under Lieutenant General Sepp Dietrich. The two Regiment Commanders of the "LAH" took command of the divisions.

From left to right: Otto Günsche; Fritz Witt, Commander of the 12th SS Armored Division "HJ"; Sepp Dietrich, Commander of the First Armored Corps; "Teddy" Wisch, Commander of the First SS Armored Division "LAH"; Max Wünsche, Regiment Commander of the 12th SS Armored Regiment "HJ".

Swearing in the young volunteers of the "HJ" Division before the Commander of the 25th SS Armored Grenadier Regiment, Kurt Meyer (known as "Panzermeyer", seen at right with Knight's Cross).

FORMATION AND TRAINING

After preliminary discussions in the spring of 1943 and the basic approval of Adolf Hitler, the latter made the appropriate decree in June of 1943. At the request of the Inspector General of the armored troops, Senior General Guderian, what was originally planned as an "Armored Grenadier Division" was changed and, on October 30, 1943, renamed the "12th SS Armored Division "Hitler Youth".

The following main training objectives were stated:
1. Physical capability
2. Character building
3. Weapons and combat training

Good weapons and equipment training was the essential requirement for service. In a fully motorized troop, the training of the drivers is particularly important.

Motorcycle gunnery training by one of the officers assigned by the army.

In rough terrain it could be seen what had been learned.

22

These pictures of practice with the 7.5 cm antitank gun of the Division Escort Company impressively demonstrate the success of the training.

Every step has been practiced countless times, and the men of the ordnance escort can do them all blindly.

In the shortest time, the sharp shot cracks out. The ordnance leader observes the accuracy.

The firepower of an armored division depends on the performance capability of the tank crews. In each tank there is often only one man with combat experience.

Training and drill continue until weapons and equipment are fully mastered. Belgian children stare at the clanking monsters.

The 12th Armored Regiment "HJ" consisted of two sections, of which the first (Major Jürgensen) was equipped with Panzer V (Panther) and the second (Battalion leader K. H. Prinz) with Panzer IV, the "workhorse" of German tanks.

24

"Let them joke, let them kiss, who knows how soon they must die..."

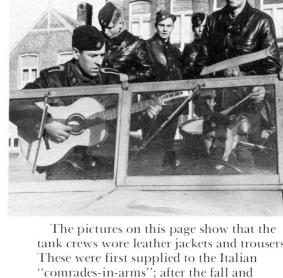

The pictures on this page show that the tank crews wore leather jackets and trousers. These were first supplied to the Italian "comrades-in-arms"; after the fall and disarmament of the Italians, in which the "LAH" played a decisive role, everything went to the armored units as "booty" and protected many of the young Panzer men from serious burns.

Combat training of the first section, 12th SS Armored Regiment. Above: Captain Wilhelm Beck supervises the training. Below: "Panther" tanks test a bridge that engineers built over the Eure at Cocherel in an hour and a half.

A training course for junior leaders and leader applicants was conducted at Evreux.

The Division Commander turns up unexpectedly again and again, assuring himself of the progress of the training.

Captain W. Beck, an experienced leader decorated with the Knight's Cross, conducted the leader applicant training. He was regarded as a reserve commander, but fell in an air raid on June 10, 1944.

On February 6, 1944, the Inspector General of the armored troops, Senior General Guderian, inspected the "HJ" Division during a training session of the 12th SS Armored Regiment "HJ", and was surprised by the progress made in its training.

From left to right: Guderian, a driver, Sepp Dietrich and Oberführer Fritz Kraemer (Chief of Staff of the First SS Armored Corps).

Sepp Dietrich and Guderian, two Panzer men with World War I experience, in discussion. They were close friends and comrades and respected each other highly.

Directing the training was the Commander of the 12th SS Armored Regiment "HJ", Lieutenant Colonel Max Wünsche, seen here in the turret of his command tank.

Reich Youth Leader Axmann, a badly wounded veteran soldier, visited the ''HJ' Division again and again (second from right above). Next to him (in HJ uniform) is one of his closest collaborators in the Reich Youth Department, Heinz John, who fell as a section leader of the Second SS Armored Regiment 12 in the fighting around Caen.

The SS Master Sergeant Terdenge of the sixth SS Armored Regiment 12 climbs aboard his Panzer IV tank in a drill.

Below: Sepp Dietrich thanks the commanders for their good training. From left to right: Monke, Bartling, Prinz, Jürgensen, H. Meyer.

INSPECTION BY FIELD MARSHAL VON RUNDSTEDT

The Supreme Commander (OB) of the West attends a drill of an "armored group" at the Beverloo Training Ground, Belgium, in March of 1944. He also spoke in praise of the training that had been accomplished in so short a time.

The OB West walks with the Division Commander in front of Regiment 25. The Chief of the 7th Company, SS Senior Company Leader Heinz Schrott, salutes with outstretched arm, while his section leader, transferred from the army, gives a military salute.

The drill was directed by Major Gerd Bremer, at that time still Commander of the III SS Armored Grenadier Regiment 26. Soon afterward he succeeded E. Olboeter as Commander of the Reconnaissance Unit of the "HJ" Division. There a young 2nd Lieutentant had shot himself after losing a "secret command item"—a painful matter, as he was the son of a Gauleiter in the NSDAP.

From left to right: Bremer, von Rundstedt, Sepp Dietrich, Mohnke. The tank in the background, equipped as a flame thrower, was no longer used in action, as the flames too often spread backward into the vehicle.

Sepp Dietrich provides the Field Marshal with field glasses. After the war von Rundstedt spoke very critically of Sepp Dietrich.

First Lieutenant Pallas informs the OB West, who watches with interest.

Commander Fritz Witt
with the upper staff of his
division.

At right Major Hubert
Meyer (Ia) with Major
Hein Springer, Division
Adjutant.

Members of the military police of the
12th SS Amored Division "HJ" with 1st
Lieutenant Kurt Buschhausen.

COLOR PHOTOS OF THE TRAINING AND SERVICE

The Commander of the 12th SS Armored Division "HJ", Brigadier General Fritz Witt, spent his 37th and last birthday, May 27, 1944, in Tillieres. The good wishes and gifts of all units showed how beloved and respected the Commander was by his men.

The model of an eight-wheel reconnaissance car obviously pleased him. (Next to Witt is Major Hein Springer, his Division Adjutant.) The color photographs, lent by his son Peter Witt, are undoubted rarities.

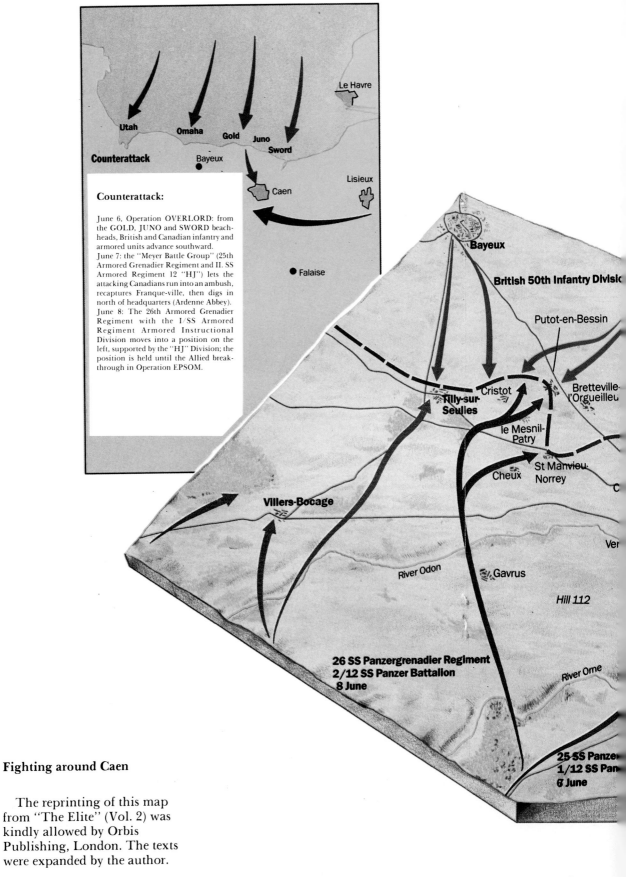

Counterattack:

June 6, Operation OVERLORD: from the GOLD, JUNO and SWORD beach-heads, British and Canadian infantry and armored units advance southward.

June 7: the "Meyer Battle Group" (25th Armored Grenadier Regiment and II. SS Armored Regiment 12 "HJ") lets the attacking Canadians run into an ambush, recaptures Franque-ville, then digs in north of headquarters (Ardenne Abbey).

June 8: The 26th Armored Grenadier Regiment with the I/SS Armored Regiment Armored Instructional Division moves into a position on the left, supported by the "HJ" Division; the position is held until the Allied break-through in Operation EPSOM.

Counterattack

Utah   Omaha   Gold   Juno   Sword

Le Havre

Bayeux

Caen   Lisieux

Falaise

British 50th Infantry Division

Putot-en-Bessin

Cristot   Bretteville-l'Orgueilleu

Tilly-sur-Seulles

le Mesnil-Patry

St Manvieu-Norrey

Cheux

Villers-Bocage

River Odon   Gavrus

Hill 112

Ver

26 SS Panzergrenadier Regiment
2/12 SS Panzer Battalion
8 June

River Orne

25 SS Panzer
1/12 Pan
7 June

Fighting around Caen

The reprinting of this map from "The Elite" (Vol. 2) was kindly allowed by Orbis Publishing, London. The texts were expanded by the author.

From Caen to Falaise:

June 26: Operation EPSOM, the Allied attempt to encircle Caen from the west, begins with the attack on Cheux and St. Manvieu. The "HJ" Division bears the brunt of this attack and is slowly pushed southward.

June 27: Units of the "HJ" Division attempt a desperate counter-attack on Cheux, but cannot recapture it and art beaten back to the slopes of Hill 112.

June 28-30: After days of hard fighting, the "HJ" Division and other divisions ("Hohenstaufen" and "Frundsberg") force the Allies to retreat from Hill 112. But the enemy remains in position south of the Ordon and makes further attacks on Hill 112 into July.

July 3: On the right flank the "HJ" Division holds the main battle line in the north of Caen, on the heights of Buron.

July 4: Operation CHARNWOOD begins with an attack on Carpiquet by the Canadians. By evening they are able to conquer the northern part of the airfield.

July 4-9: The "HJ" Division is driven back from Buron and suffers severe losses in an attempt to stop the Allied advance on Caen.

July 11: The "HJ" Division is transferred to Potigny for regrouping.

July 18-20: After Allied attempts, in the framework of Operation GOODWOOD, to break through the German lines from the northeast, the "HJ" Division is thrown into battle again south of Caen.

August 7-20: Operation TOTALIZE. The remains of the "HJ" Division fight in constant opposition to the Allies who are attacking along the road to Falaise, and hold the northern part of the enclosing ring near Falaise open for several days.

August 20: "Panzermeyer" withdraws over the Dives with the survivors of the "HJ" Division.

Legend

 Armored Instruction Division

 2nd Armored Division

 12th SS Armored Division "HJ"

✪ Tactical Command Post "HJ"

★ Division Command Post

▲ Artillery Positions of the "HJ" Division

 Allied Positions

— — Main Battle Line until Operation EPSOM

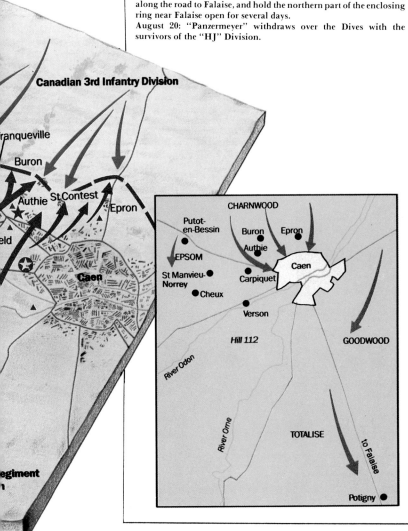

One of the many freight aircraft of the 6th British Airborne Division, destroyed on the ground in the Caen area, where the British landed behind the German lines.

Below: A Spitfire shot down on the coast—one of the feared fighter-bombers fewer.

The burning remains of a Spitfire just shot down in the "HJ" Division's battleground around Caen.

These young soldiers held their positions in the trenches tenaciously, defying all attacks by the enemy who was so very superior in numbers and materials.

Junior leaders and men of the 12th SS Armored Division "HJ". The relentless fighting has already left its traces on the young faces.

Major Hans Waldmüller, with his I/25 Battalion, held the right flank position of the "HJ" Division for weeks against the hardest attacks, under constant fire from naval artillery. For that he was honored with the Knight's Cross on August 27, 1944. On September 8, 1944 he was tricked into an ambush, murdered and dreadfully mutilated by Belgian partisans near Basse-Bodeux. He found his last resting place in the Heroes' Cemetery in Düren.

Waldmüller's Adjutant, SS 2nd Lieutenant Willi Klein, in a camouflaged position near Cambes.

Munitions are brought forward past the wreck of an enemy tank.

A Sherman tank put out of action in the defensive fighting around Caen.

This attempt to shoot down aircraft with an MG 42 could scarcely have been successful against the armored fighter-bombers.

At Ardenne Abbey, regimental command post of the 25th Armored Grenadier Regimental Commander, 1st Lieutenant Heinz Milius, with the Ia of the "HJ" Division, Hubert Meyer, behind them, with the "golden HJ Division, Hubert Meyer, behind them, with the "golden HJ emblem" the war correspondent Herbert Reinecker, and at right Senior Company Leader Meitzel, the 01.

Ardenne Abbey in the summer of 1984.

Those who fell were generally buried first at the site in the blood-drenched soil of Normandy. During the few pauses in the battle, members of the division cared for the graves of their fallen comrades.

After the war the remains were transferred to large military cemeteries, in which the former enemies often lie side by side in their last rest. Here, in that of La Cambe, lie more than 21,000 dead.

During an inspection of the battlefields, the veterans of the "HJ" Division visit the graves of their comrades. The men of the 12th SS Armored Regiment "HJ" paused at the grave of their fallen commander and buried Captain Michael Wittmann, whose remains had been found just shortly before, with his tank crew at La Cambe. The former Ia Hubert Meyer gave the memorial address, in the company of a French colonel, family members, and the men of the Second Unit, Armored Regiment and the Third Battalion, Armored Grenadier Regiment 26.

A British Sherman
tank in a defensive
position near Caen.
The picture below
shows corpsmen of
the Fourth Canadian
Armoured Division
south of Caen at the
end of July,
preparing for
Operation Totalize.

The color photos
on this page were
reproduced from the
book "Normandie
Album Memorial"
with the kind
permission of
Editions Heimdal.

After the removal of the tank's turret, a new armored transport vehicle for infantrymen was created and named "Kangaroo".

A noteworthy Canadian infantryman smokes a cigarette with a military policeman of the Second Canadian Division, while sitting under a road sign left by his German "colleagues" (August 18 in Falaise).

Former members of the Second
SS Armored Regiment 12 with
their Unit Commander Siegel
and the Ia of the "HJ" Division,
Hubert Meyer, in front of the
Musee Memorial de la Bataille in
Bayeux. Also seen in front of this
museum, which is well worth
visiting and fair to both sides, are
the author and a French
historian.

Left: title page of a Sunday
Express edition on the 40th
anniversary of the invasion.

D-DAY—THEY ARE COMING!

Within a short time, these words turned into firm concepts, which both described the situation and almost became a cliche, just as did the quotation by Field Marshal Rommel: "This is the longest day."

This "long day" began on June 6, 1944, when Allied paratroopers were landed even before midnight. The masses of troops landed in the early morning hours of this day that can be said to have decided the war. They came with an armada that, in its size, far exceeded all German hopes and fears.

It still seems incomprehensible today that German intelligence had noticed nothing of the vast preparations, and that individual precise reports from the German command posts were ignored. In any case, though, a scarcely imaginable confusion prevailed in the realm of subordination conditions and commands.

British soldiers board the landing craft "Empire Lance" in Southampton on May 29, 1944.

British soldiers board the landing craft "Empire Lance" in Southampton on May 29, 1944.

Montgomery declared long before the landing: "Our advantages are based on surprise and initiative. We command a mighty firepower of several thousand warships, and 10,500 war planes will fly above them constantly. Our invasion troops (130,000 men on day X) are well prepared and burning with desire to fight. Nothing comparable has ever been seen."

Only those soldiers of the "HJ" Division who frequently slipped through the enemy positions, and often came only as far as the coast, had this view. The situation underscores an utterance of Senior General Guderian, who said to Hitler: "The bravery of the armored troops alone is not in a position to make up for the lack of two parts of our armed forces—the Air Force and the Navy."

These pictures show how
untroubled by the
possibility of German air
attacks the Allies were when
they set their troops on
shore. Above: a British
armored column, at its head
a "Cromwell IV" of the 7th
British Armoured Division.
This unit, known as the
"Desert Rats" because of
their success in Africa, was
later shot down in Villers-
Bocage, chiefly by the
single Tiger tank of
Captain Wittmann. Right:
troops of the 3rd Infantry
Division await their
marching orders.

Right: paratroopers and air-landed troops who landed the night before June 6, 1944 secure the crossings of the Orne. Below: British infantry seeks cover from German sharpshooters behind a Mark 10 Tank Destroyer.

BAPTISM OF FIRE

When events lie so far in the past, more than forty years ago, it is not impossible that faulty memories or wrong interpretations of what happened can unavoidably lead to errors in the portrayal of the course of events. This can also happen because most of the data at hand are incomplete, or because errors have been made in transmitting the data. In translating texts from a foreign language, further errors are added, which one chronicler copies from another.

I shall try to describe the first action of the "HJ" as it has remained in my memory.

The II. Unit, SS Armored Regiment 12 "HJ", was alerted in the night of June 4-5, 1944 and mobilized so that the armored companies, three or four vehicles of each remaining in the quarters near Elbeuf, met the units of Armored Grenadier Regiment 25 during the course of the day, sometimes only toward evening. On June 6, 1944, a maneuver drill was to be carried out within the division.

In the night before June 6 there was unusual aircraft activity, and toward morning it was certain: "They are coming!"

The day for which the young soldiers of the "HJ" Division had waited was breaking.

The soldiers in the battle units knew nothing of the confusion of commands in the higher staffs, of which one can read in the historical studies of the war.

At first the units marched in the direction of Lisieux, but they were turned toward the west later. Thus the units reached the city of Caen only deep in the night, some arriving only early the next morning.

Panzer IV of the 2nd Unit, SS Armored Regiment 12 "HJ", on the march to the invasion front.

Around noon of June 7, approximately fifty Panzer IV were on hand. It must be remembered here that the tanks had been underway for many hours and kilometers, with all the resulting technical problems. The young tank drivers slept sitting up at every stop. When the tanks arrived, they were placed in a great semicircular defensive line north of the Caen-Bayeux road. In this way the enemy was to be hindered from taking the important Carpiquet airfield and penetrating into the city of Caen.

The leader of the battle group, Colonel Kurt Meyer, known as "Panzermeyer", Commander of SS Armored Grenadier Regiment 25, set up his command post at Ardenne Abbey. The building with its strong arches offered protection and cover. From the towers and a gallery running around the roof one had a good view as far as the coast, which the roof one had a good view as far as the coast, which was marked by barrage balloons of the Allied landing fleet.

The enemy attack took place as expected. Standing under cover on the gallery, Colonel Meyer and liaison officers observed the enemy forces, tanks and infantry, as they advanced closer and closer to our Panzer IV tanks standing in ambush positions. All involved parties, including myself, followed the events almost as if from the balconies of a theater, acoustically underscored by the announcements via radio. The drama became a tragedy for the British when, on the command "Fire at will!", our tanks fired as one. Immediately numerous enemy tanks burst into flames. Surprised and confused, others drove every which way across the battlefield. The closed attack of our tanks was successful in this chaos.

The main entrance to Ardenne Abbey.

Artillery observers utilize the broad view from the towers of Ardenne Abbey.

7.5 cm antitank gun ready to fire in ambush position.

Major Karl Heinz Prinz, born February 28, 1914, Knight's Cross on July 11, 1944, fallen August 14, 1944.

Discussion of the artillery support by Major K. H. Prinz, II SS Armored Regiment 12, with the artillery commanders, Urbanitz and Bartling, in Ardenne Abbey.

A young Panzer grenadier of SS Armored Grenadier Regiment 25 awaits the attack.

The leader of the tanks was the Commander of the Second SS Armored Regiment 12 "HJ", Major Karl Heinz Prinz, an experienced tank fighter and tactician, but it soon became obvious that he could no longer reach the individual companies by radio. For me this meant that I was no longer a "spectator", but had to try to maintain contact with the armored companies in an amphibian vehicle.

The relentless advance of the tanks—meanwhile the rest of the unit had attacked on the flank—was nevertheless soon halted by the opposition of the enemy, who had set up more and more strong and reinforced antitank barriers.

Shortly thereafter, the Division was given its first lesson in what was to be our fate in the coming weeks, when the rain of fire began in unexpected measure, with a concentration of material such as would scarcely be seen again in such a relatively limited area in the whole of World War II. Although the enemy's artillery was far superior to ours in numbers, excellently situated and aimed with the help of observation aircraft ("invasion gnats"), and though the fighter-bombers attacked steadily, one factor still remains unforgettable to all participants: that the fleet lying just off the coast battered the Division thunderously with its highest-caliber naval artillery. The whistling of the approaching heavy shells and the explosions as they struck had a devastating effect.

The Division Commander, Brigadier General Fritz Witt, is always in close contact with his troops; here with "Panzermeyer" and Max Wünsche at Ardenne Abbey.

Left: underway with "Panzermeyer" as driver and Dd. Gatternick in the sidecar.

Below: with Lieutenant General Sepp Dietrich, observing enemy aircraft.

Preparing for a counterattack with mortar support.

The grenadier in the foreground is carrying the heavy barrel of the 8 cm mortar.

A heavy burden: the base of the mortar on the back of the man at far left.

Last test of the weapons.

The SS Armored
Grenadier
Regiment 26
Colonel W.
Mohnke) had an
approach route of
about 160 km, twice
as long as that of its
sister Regiment 25.
The latter was
hindered by the
aerial superiority of
the enemy and the
civilians fleeing
from the battle area.

Thus these units met only on June 8 and later in the area around Caen and were placed to the left, next to Regiment 25.

Grenadiers of a subordinate military unit are briefed by the leaders of the "HJ" Division.

The Third Company of Armored Regiment 12 "HJ" had the misfortune of having to go into battle without their experienced Commander Rudolf von Ribbentrop, as he had been injured by fighter-bomber fire during a maneuver drill shortly before. He released himself from the hospital and drove to the invasion front, where he too had to watch his company being shattered.

A captain transferred from the army led the battle staff in the attack on Norrey and culpably neglected the free right flank. As soon as the tanks entered open country, the entire leading column of five tanks was blasted by camouflaged antitank fire. Two additional "Panthers" of the Company joined in, one of which exploded from within.

The attack was aborted as soon as its hopelessness was recognized. The crews that had lost their tanks attempted to take cover despite heavy machine-gun fire. The Company's ranking medical officer, Siegfried Goose, came to the aid of his comrades, some of whom were badly burned, but he was fatally struck by a burst of machine-gun fire. The "experienced tank captain" suffered a nervous shock, and Rudolf von Ribbentrop, despite being wounded, took command of what remained of the Company and held the left corner position of the "HJ" Division for several days, next to the Armored Instructional Division.

On June 14 the sad statistics were added up: 18 dead and 33 injured. Only four tanks were still usable. These were turned over to other units and the Third Company was withdrawn for reassignment.

The fact that the "Panther" could catch fire quickly was attributed to the hydraulic fluid in the steering system. A few days later a "Panther" caught fire immediately from a hit on its bow plate that did not break through the armor at all.

Later, when an experienced English tank sergeant was taken prisoner, he made a show of turning away before striking a match. When asked why, he said with a wink of his eye that it was better to look all around in case a "Panther" was in the vicinity, as it would burn and explode immediately.

Lieutenant Colonel von Ribbentrop, in infantry uniform without Knight's Cross, in the sidecar. The motorcycle is driven by Regiment Commander Wünsche.

The English antitank guns could be camouflaged easily in the terrain that was inherently very unfavorable to tanks, and were much feared by our tank crews. This gun emplacement of the 5/7th Gordon Highlanders had already destroyed two Panzer IV tanks.

On the other hand, the British had great respect for the German minefields. With a special device mounted in front of a tank, they made the mines explode.

The British tanks move forward within the course marked by white lines.

The sign at the right side of the field indicates that this attack sector has been cleared of mines.

The dead of both sides were first buried in the blood-drenched earth of Normandy.
Below: at the grave of a fallen tank soldier are his comrades and an Anglican pastor,
June 7, 1944.

Men of Armored Grenadier Regiment 25 erect temporary grave crosses for the dead along the walls of Ardenne Abbey during the first days.

Correspondent-photographer Woscidlo went into no-man's land with a group of volunteers to photograph the grave of a young grenadier for his parents.

Because of the numerical superiority in personnel and materials, the losses in dead and wounded in the 12th SS Armored Division "Hitler Youth" were very high. Especially vital, and incomprehensible to many, was the death of the Division Commander, Brigadier General Fritz Witt. When his headquarters came under heavy fire from naval artillery, he saw to it that his men got under cover, and was struck fatally, along with three members of his staff.

Above: one of the last photographs of Fritz Witt with Max Wünsche (left) and "Panzermeyer" (right).

Left: Colonel Kurt Meyer took command of the "HJ" Division. Soon thereafter he was promoted to Oberführer, and on August 21, 1944, he was the 91st soldier to be decorated with the Iron Cross.

In Rottach-Egern, his family's place of residence, a memorial service for the fallen Commander of the "HJ" Division was held. The population honored the worthy soldier by their participation in large numbers.

The insignia of the "LAH" and leaders of the armored regiment precede the honor guard of the Tölz Officer School, with volunteers from all divisions of the Waffen SS from many European lands.

From right to left: Lieutenant General Baron von Eberstein, Mrs. Witt, son Peter Witt, Major Klingenberg (Commandant of the Tölz Officer School), on his lap the oldest daughter of Fritz Witt (he left five children).

Fighter-bombers Attack!

At first scarcely recognizable as small spots in the sky, the fighter-bombers were suddenly there, flying low over the hedges and drawing a row of fire through the landscape of Normandy.

The photograph below shows what power was thus unleashed.

Driving safely past a column that had been hit by the fighter-bombers was always a victory. At any moment a portion of the munitions could explode.

This armored vehicle tows another away, past a burning vehicle.

The only protection against fighter-bombers was complete camouflage. At first scarcely nothing in this picture is recognizable. Thus the purpose was fulfilled.

Again and again the fighter-bombers attacked columns that should have been protected by displaying the Red Cross. The pictures on this page can only hint at what happened here.

And when a fighter-bomber was shot down from the skies, it is understandable that the foot-soldiers did not exactly receive the shot-down pilots very hospitably.

The photo at right, though, shows just the opposite. At left in the picture is Correspondent Wolfgang Pahl, at right Photographer W. Woscidlo, who took the greater part of the "HJ" Division's combat photos.

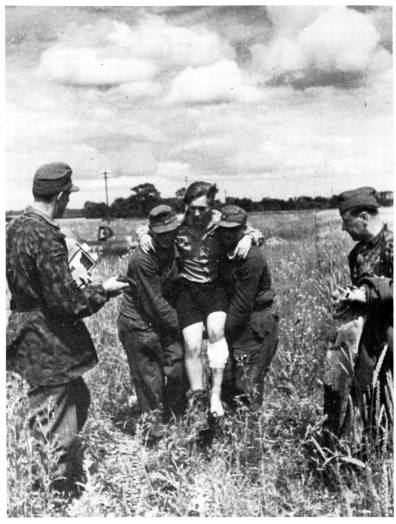

BOMBS ON CAEN

Report of the bomb attack of July 7, 1944 on the German positions north of Caen, in preparation for the offensive out of the beachhead (Operation Charnwood):

Reporter: the then Company Commander of the 8th Company, Armored Regiment 12 "HJ", First Lieutenant Herbert Höfler. Recorded from the memory of an eyewitness in July of 1987.

The 8th Company, Armored Regiment 12, with its approximately twelve Panzer IV tanks then serviceable, was in position northwest of Caen, on the heights at the old water tower, and westward to Ardenne Abbey.

It was a warm summer evening with a clear sky. We heard the roar of a group of four-engine bombers flying toward us from the coast, and observed the flight of the approximately 250 to 300 craft. Suddenly "Pathfinder Machines" spread out and lit beacons of light over our position.

I commanded: "All crews into the tanks—hatches closed—greatest caution—observation to all sides."

Seconds later the inferno broke out over us. The next ten to fifteen minutes seemed like an eternity to us."

SS 1st Lieutenant Herbert Höfler.

A "Panther" tries to find a way through the ruins of Caen.

Since a great percentage of the bombs fell not on the positions of German troops but on the northern part of the city, the inhabitants of Caen literally ran for their lives and had to watch their city's destruction helplessly.

Fountains of earth and dust made it impossible to see anything. The tanks vibrated and were sometimes pushed aside. Splinters and clods of earth rained endlessly down on the army vehicles.

All of a sudden the haunting was at an end.

At first nothing at all was to be seen in the dust and smoke. Then we could tell that we stood amid a gray-brown landscape of craters. Hedges, bushes, even the grass had disappeared, the tanks were covered over and over with branches and pieces of metal.

Losses: two Panzer IV, from direct hits, seven dead and four wounded. Two tanks had slid down into deep bomb craters and could be hauled out only with difficulty.

The army vehicles were immediately cleaned of earth and rubble, weapons, equipment and motors were cleaned to be ready for use again. During the night the ordnance officers of the unit were able to get through to us and direct the company through the city by adventurous routes into a new position.

The whole extent of the bomb damage could be seen the next morning. It became clear that even tanks could get through the rubble only with the help of engineers.

Below: grenadiers of the "HJ" Division in the forecourt of the railroad station.

"One takes a last look back
at the burial place of his
belongings."

As always, bombing war strikes those
most easily wounded. Mothers try to
rescue their children from the chaos.

The fighter-bombers attack everything that moves, and thus civilians are also hit, such as this woman who asks the German soldiers for help.

Those who are presumably better off try to salvage at least a part of their belongings, but that often ends in the gutter.

Tanks were vulnerable from the air to a great degree. For this reason the armored units were equipped more and more with anti-aircraft guns on tank chassis. The SS Armored Regiment 12 "HJ" had 2 cm anti-aircraft guns mounted on the very fast and nimble Panzer 38 (t). Their weaponry, though, was sadly inferior to that of the attacking fighter-bombers, and succeeded only through unexpected, fast and accurate shooting.

This picture shows that in spite of the odds, noteworthy successes were achieved. The Commander of the SS Armored Regiment 12 "HJ", Max Wünsche, decorates a mobile gun driver with the Iron Cross for shooting down five aircraft. In the middle of the picture is Radio Officer Schlauss.

Karl Wilhelm Krause, at left, as 2nd Lieutenant and orderly in the main headquarters, at right as Commander and leader of the anti-aircraft forces of the 2nd Unit, SS Armored Regiment 12, "HJ".

He had the idea of mounting the three four-barrel 2 cm anti-aircraft guns of his section on old Panzer IV chassis. For this unique experiment he had the support of his superior officers, and with the help of the Workshop Company Chief he created a completely new weapon. It shot down 27 aircraft and also gave good support during armored attacks.

Hitler was so inspired by the new weapon that he ordered all armored units to be equipped as quickly as possible with these mobile guns, known as "Whirlwind".

Preparations for an attack at the Allied staff headquarters.

With their piper in the lead, these Highlanders march into position.

Attack with armored support in the half-light of dawn.

This English soldier certainly does not yet know what he will face on this day.

The attacking grenadiers were always in contact with the supporting heavy weapons via "Walkie-Talkie".

Again and again there was intense fighting in the small towns of Normandy. Every foot of ground in the burning ruins was bitterly contested.

The "Bren Gun" was very inferior to the German MG 42 as a light machine gun. Its typical slow shooting speed often provided sound orientation for the penetration of the British troops.

With guns at the ready, protecting them on all sides, these British grenadiers move cautiously farther forward.

Everyone cooperated in caring for the wounded and transporting them to field hospitals as quickly as possible. No one knew when it would be his turn to depend on the help and care of his comrades.

This drawing by an SS Armored Corps artist shows the move to a field hospital of the "HJ" Division in the northern part of Caen. The capable field doctors were on duty day and night. Many of them were highly honored, and deserved to be.

Help for the wounded was naturally given to the enemy too.

In the upper picture, a German medic cares for Canadian soldiers. At right, a "Tommy" bandages a wounded German armored corpsman.

IMPRISONMENT

There is scarcely a soldier who considers the possibility of becoming a prisoner of war. These pictures show the bewilderment and blank looks, even the fear of an unknown fate.

Members of the "Hitler Youth" Division, wounded, are taken prisoner.

Though the lower picture indicates that prisoners from the "Hitler Youth" Division were properly treated and their belongings inspected, the picture above shows that, alas, serious mistreatment also took place.

THE OPPONENTS
AND THE BATTLEFIELD

The British had very fast and handy scout cars. Two prisoners from the 16th Air Force Field Division were transported on this four-wheel scout car.

The burning wreckage of a destroyed British scout car.

Captured scout cars were used gladly by German troops. An M-8 Greyhound is shown here.

Infantrymen are brought forward to the front sitting on Sherman tanks.

The British "Bren Carriers" were ideal for the terrain of Normandy. They could be used in many ways, including as light artillery tractors.

British tanks (7th Armoured Division) roll through the ruins to attack Tilly sur Seules.

Below: a Sherman M4 AT "Firefly" in position.

A Panther of the 3rd
SS Armored Regiment 12
ready to counterattack.

On the way into
action, air observation
was especially important
and indispensible.

Pauses in the fighting were very seldom on both sides, and were probably used in different ways.
Above: a little music at the position of the 3rd SS Armored Regiment 25 near Buron.
Below: soldiers of the 5th/7th Gordon Highlanders have a tea break.

The Commander of the 1st Armored Grenadier Regiment 25, Major
Waldmüller, directs men to their stations. (At left is Correspondent Pahl.)

Armored Grenadiers of Regiment 25 in a ditch north of Caen.

The young grenadiers held out in their foxholes for days and weeks, holding off the enemy's ever-repeated attacks.

These were the brave defenders of Caen. One awaits the enemy with his bazooka.

At right: ready to spring into a counterattack.

Below: a particularly successful group was decorated with the Iron Cross II.

This amateur photo was taken from a Panzer IV in its defensive position at Height 112. This commanding high point was hotly contested, and was referred to by the Canadians as "Calvary".

Group pictures of men and leaders of the 2nd SS Armored Regiment 12 in their unit's battle stationsjust below Height 112. It is interesting that the four 2nd Lieutenants (Kommadina, Porsch, Walther and Freitag) all wear different uniforms.

The British Prime Minister, Winston Churchill, was very interested in the progress of the invasion fighting and frequently crossed the Channel to see for himself on the spot. Here he is informed as to the situation by Montgomery.

BBC Correspondent Chester Wilmot, talking here with the men of a French commando unit, accompanied the attacking forces. Because of his widely respected radio reporting, in which he always emphasized the extraordinary bravery of the "Hitler Youth" Division, he contributed to the almost legendary reputation they enjoy to this day.

British soldiers in front of the Cook Travel Bureau after their conquest of Caen. Their crossing was surely not booked by that firm.

Preparation for a counterattack by the 1st SS Armored Grenadier Regiment 26.
Above: the Commander, Major Bernhard Krause, points the way to one of his leaders.

Below: grenadiers whose faces mirror the seriousness of the situation await the command to attack.

Sufficient support by heavy weapons was, unfortunately, possible only in the rarest cases. The lack of ammunition during extended fighter-bomber attacks on supply lines and the crushing enemy superiority in long-range weapons, that struck all positions, were the reasons.

The 22nd Armoured Brigade, part of the 7th Armoured Division, battle-tested in Africa, tried on June 13, 1944 to make a bold move forward to occupy the important road junction at Villers-Bocage far behind the troops fighting around Caen.

They had the misfortune to meet the SS Armored Regiment Unit 501 "LAH", just called up from the hinterlands. The ruins of the shattered unit testify to the violence of the battle.

The battle around Villers-Bocage cost the life of the German army's most successful armored commander, SS 1st Lieutenant Michel Wittmann. He began by driving his "Tiger" tank alone against the completely amazed "Desert Foxes" and shooting down 25 armored vehicles. When he fell shortly thereafter, on August 8, 1944, he had brought down a total of 138 enemy armored vehicles and 132 antitank guns.

When one compares these pictures, it scarcely seems possible that a colossal tank like the Tiger, which was thought to be practically unbeatable, could be blown apart in such a manner.

In the case of this tank it has never been determined to this day how it could have been tipped over and destroyed in this way.

109

Upper left: Major Karl Heinz Prinz, who was one of the first of the "HJ" Division to be decorated with the Knight's Cross in recognition of the 2nd SS Armored Division 12's achievements.

Right: Master Sergeant Richard Rudolf, who earned the Knight's Cross while a section leader in the 9th SS Armored Regiment 12. As did Corporal Fritz Eckstein, he came from the Armored Fusilier Company of the LAH, led by Prinz (see below). In addition, 1st Lieutenant G. Hurdelbrink and Senior Platoon Leader Rudi Roy of the old "Prinz Company" earned the Knight's Cross on the invasion front.

From left to right: Eckstein, Krämer, Sepp Dietrich, Bernhard Krause, Hugo Kraas.

On November 15, 1944 Colonel Hugo Kraas took command of the 12th SS Armored Division "Hitler Youth". From the men who had survived the fighting around Caen and the battles during their retreat from France he formed a new unit and commanded it successfully until the end in 1945.

Pictures from his life as a soldier: Above: at right in the picture as company chief in Russia, summer, 1941.
Left: After being accorded the Knight's Cross as Major and Commander of the First Battalion, SS Armored Grenadier Regiment 2 "LAH" (March 28, 1943).
Below: as a Colonel in the Führer's headquarters after being decorated with the oak leaf cluster to the Knight's Cross in January of 1944.

THE ARDENNES OFFENSIVE

Only portions of the 12th SS Armored Division "Hitler Youth" saw service in the Ardennes offensive; for a long time the vacancies had not all been filled, and materials were lacking everywhere.

During the new formation, a delegation of the 8th SS Armored Regiment 12 was invited to visit Economic Minister Funk in Berlin. In the middle of the picture are the leaders: Siegel (with Knight's Cross), Kändler, Traude and Höfler (previously Funk's adjutant).

The Commander of the 2nd SS Armored Regiment 12, Captain Hans Siegel, was transferred from the reorganization in Fallingbostel to the front to take command of what remained of the Armored Regiment 12 "HJ". His men prepared a "damply merry" farewell for him.

SERVICE IN HUNGARY

In March of 1945 the 12th Armored Division "Hitler Youth" was thrown into battle in Hungary. Tanks and armored units are shown on the march toward Plattensee.

The advance had to be broken off after heavy losses.

What remained of the Division, moved farther and farther back through the Vienna Woods; tanks were scarcely available any more, and the few surviving tank corpsmen fought as infantry. The last, costly defensive fighting near Hirtenberg made possible the march over the demarcation line on the Enns to become American prisoners.

As one of the last, Captain Leader Werner Damsch received the Knight's Cross on April 17, 1945 as Commander of the 1st SS Armored Grenadier Regiment 25.

SERVICE RECORD

Established in the summer of 1943 at the Belgian training camp of Beverloo

1944	Service in the West
April/June	OKW Reserve in Evreux-Laigle-Dreux area
June/ November	Fighting on the invasion front in Normandy, Caen area.
	Heavy losses in the Falaise basin
	Retreat via Argentan, Dreux, Rouen, Hirson, through Belgium into German territory
	Reorganization (with replacements from the Air Force and Navy) in the Sauerland and the area around Nienburg on the Weser
December to 1945 January	Costly advance via Bullingen in the Eupen-Malmedy area (Ardennes offensive)
	Fighting on the front at Bastogne
	Retreat into the Eifel Mountains
	Transfer to Hungary
	Service in the East
February/ May	Fighting at Gran bridgehead, near Stuhlweissenburgand on the Plattensee
	Costly fighting and retreat via Oedenburg into the Vienna Woods
	Defensive fighting near Hirtenberg
	After the surrender, march back over the Enns into the Linz area

AMERICAN PRISONERS